Wibber Dibber Doo

I love you!

Written by Kaye Saoirse Pearse

Illustrated by Rebekah Wells

DEDICATION

Dedicated to Angela, who called my little story "magical" and encouraged me to share it with the world.

And to Taylor, always in my heart.

ACKNOWLEDGMENTS

Published with the assistance and cooperation of Jennie Shuklis and the staff, volunteers, and Board of Directors of the Fluvanna County SPCA, a no-kill shelter in Troy, Virginia.

A portion of the proceeds from the sale of this book will be donated to the shelter.

Printed using the Architect's Daughter© typeface, courtesy of KG Fonts

On a crisp Autumn day, in a nearby town,

A woman walked into a shelter, feeling down.

"My much-loved cat died and my heart is sad,

Do you have any cats who can make me feel glad?"

"Yes, yes!" said the worker, "we have cats galore.

Cats who will love you. Cats you will adore.

Orange cats, black cats, white cats and more.

They're all in that room. Go in and explore!"

So the woman explored, she saw cats large and small.

She wanted to be sure she visited them all.

But none of the kitties, not orange, black or white,

None of the kitties was exactly quite right.

She feared she would find no cat there for her,

Then she spied a small fluffball of gray and white fur.

"Look, look!" The woman exclaimed in surprise,

"This little kitten has diamond-shaped eyes!"

"He does," said the worker, "he's quite special you know!

When he was a baby, he was scared and so,

I'd put on my shirt, and inside it he would go,

And I carried him everywhere, to and fro."

R WELLS 15

The woman took the diamond-eyed kitten home that day,

And his new Meowmy discovered that he loved to play.

He jumped on the chairs, he hid under tables.

He sat on the computer and nibbled at its cables.

He dashed behind the sofa where he found a toy mouse

That he carried in his teeth all over the house.

He played 'til toys on the floor were all strewed,

He didn't stop until he heard Meowmy pour him some food.

He was so hungry that he climbed up Meowmy's back,

Then jumped on the counter and ate right from the sack!

Meowmy chuckled and said "No serious name for silly little you.

I'm going to call my playful boy, 'Wibber Dibber Doo'!"

After eating, he ran off to play with a ball,

Which sparkled and jingled and bounced off the wall.

It landed in the tub and Wibber jumped in after,

'Round and 'round he chased it, to the sound of Meowmy's laughter.

He stopped when, above him, he saw something white,

It flittered and fluttered and danced in the light.

He jumped up and grabbed it and down the hall he whirled,

A roll of paper waving behind him, like a flag unfurled.

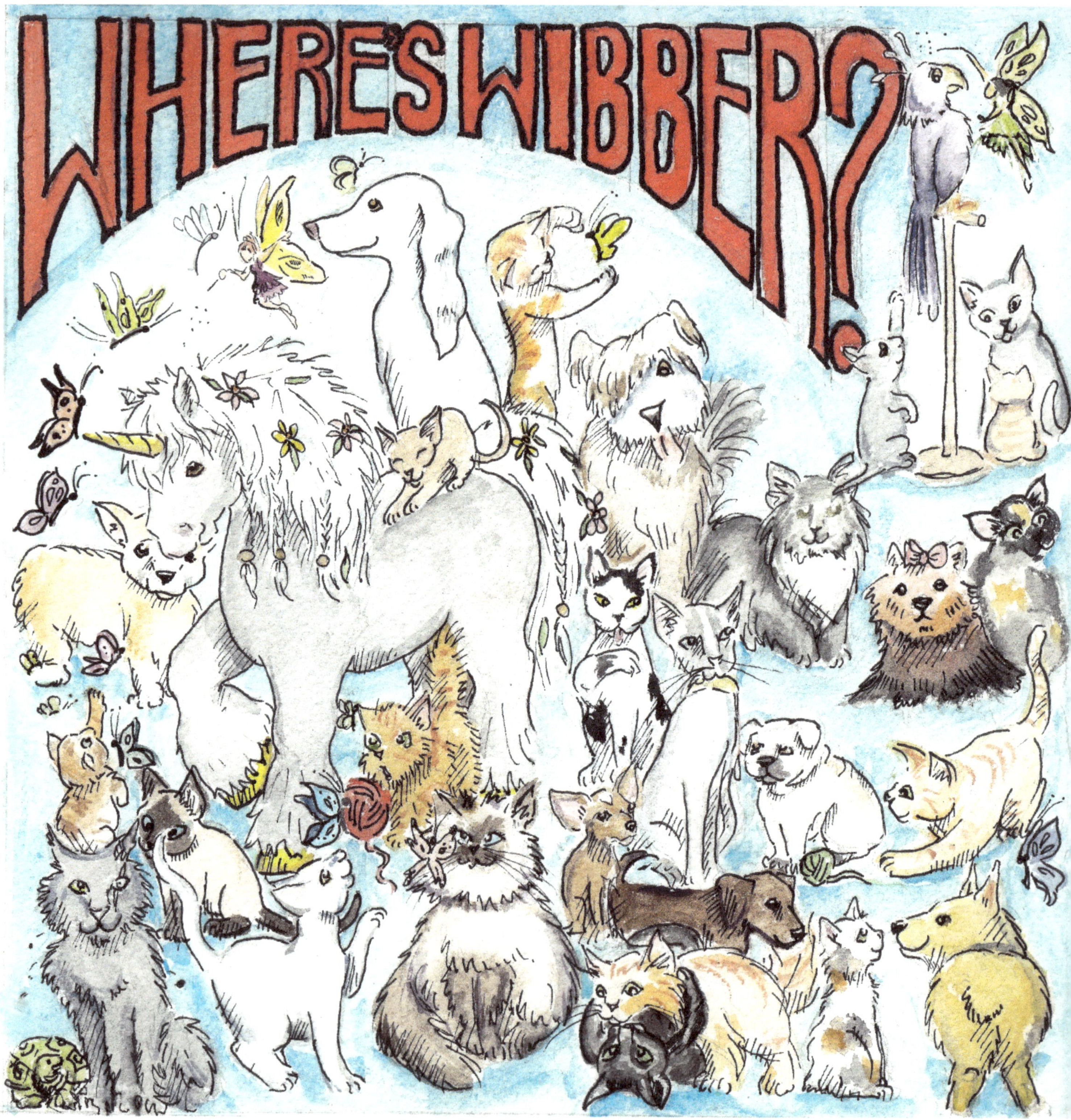
WHERE'S WIBBER?

Then Wibber saw his Meowmy cleaning out the wood stove,

And when she turned her back, inside it he dove.

When he hopped out again, he was covered in soot,

From the tip of his tail to the pads on each foot.

After cleaning his pawpads, he jumped on the bed,

Right on top of dawgie Boo, who raised her shaggy head.

She sniffed him, then licked him, and without a yap,

They curled up together for an afternoon nap.

He woke when from the kitchen he heard a rumble.

Meowmy had pushed a button and created a tumble

Of ice crystals all shiny and glittery.

Some missed her glass and hit the floor all skittery.

Wibber tried to catch them as down they pelted,

He wanted to play, but they too-quickly melted.

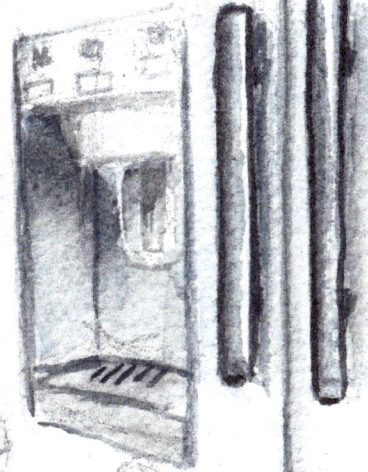

So Wibber walked away 'til 'round the door he was peeping,

And into the next room he started stealthily creeping.

Then with a flounce and a bounce, and a straight-legged leap,

Wibber pounced on sister Lola, who was sound asleep.

Lola woke with a start. She growled and hissed.

But before she could scratch him, Wibber leapt off with a twist.

As Meowmy watched in shock, up the curtains he scurried.

She ran to him saying, "Come down, I'm so worried!"

But Wibber kept climbing and ignored her cries,

Then watched from the curtaintop with his diamond-shaped eyes.

She knew she should be strict, she knew she should scold him.

But Meowmy couldn't resist just wanting to hold him.

To cradle him in her arms and to warmly enfold him.

So she scooped him up and onto his back she rolled him.

He started to wriggle, and he started to mew,

But she snuggled him close and began to coo.

So he tucked his little head up under her chin,

Then on his new Meowmy's face there spread a wide grin.

And he purred when he heard, for he knew it was true,

"Wibber Dibber Doo -- I love you!"

ABOUT THE AUTHOR

Kaye Saoirse Pearse is a graduate of the University of Georgia, and has a Master's Degree in Education from the City University of New York. A middle school teacher, she now resides on acreage in Central Virginia with an assortment of animals, including Wibber, the diamond-eyed cat. She has previously been published in the anthologies, "Dear Wonderful You" and "#FlipTheScript", and written for the online newspaper, *The Guardian*.

ABOUT THE ARTIST

Rebekah Wells is an illustrator who lives with her husband in Staffordshire, England, and has been drawing and painting since she was two years old. When not drawing, she is an active medieval re-enactor, where she sews, embroiders and, not surprisingly, does illuminations. And, while her house is currently without cats, she is looking for the ideal cat and holds out hope that, one day soon, one will choose them to be their forever home.

ABOUT WIBBER DIBBER DOO

Wibber was adopted from the Fluvanna County SPCA shelter in October, 2014. He was born with a condition known as eyelid agenesis and needed corrective surgery at a very young age. His amazing diamond-shaped eyes are the result of that surgery! The wonderful shelter workers arranged to have the procedure done, and then nursed and nurtured him until he was old enough to come home with his new Meowmy.

ABOUT THE Fluvanna SPCA

The Fluvanna Society for the Prevention of Cruelty to Animals is a 501(c)(3) nonprofit organization that was founded in 1989. Its stated mission is to rescue domestic animals from cruelty, neglect, and abandonment and to place them in good, loving, permanent homes.
http://fspca.org/

Adopt a shelter pet, and find your own story!

www.ingramcontent.com/pod-product-compliance
Lightning Source LLC
LaVergne TN
LVHW072054070426
835508LV00002B/85